Tricky Nickys
Chocolate Custard

BERNADETTE GILLIGAN

First published 2017

© 2017 Bernadette Gilligan

The moral right of the author has been asserted. All rights reserved. Without limiting the rights under copyright restricted above, no part of this publication may be reproduced, stored in or introduced into a retrieval system, or transmitted, in any form or by any means (electronic, mechanical, photocopying, recording or otherwise), without the prior written permission of both the copyright owner and the above publisher of this book.

This book is a work of fiction. Names, characters, places and incidents are a product of the Author's imagination, or if real, are used in a fictitious context.

A Cataloguing-in-Publication record is available from the National Library of Australia.

ISBN: 978-0-6480988-1-2

Illustrated by Liz Imbriano

This book is dedicated to my five adult children Jai, Dean, Aaron, Nicholas, and Jenae and my 6 grandchildren, Chloe-Jade, Izabella-Jade, Cayden, Tayah, Mason, Leon and the many more to come

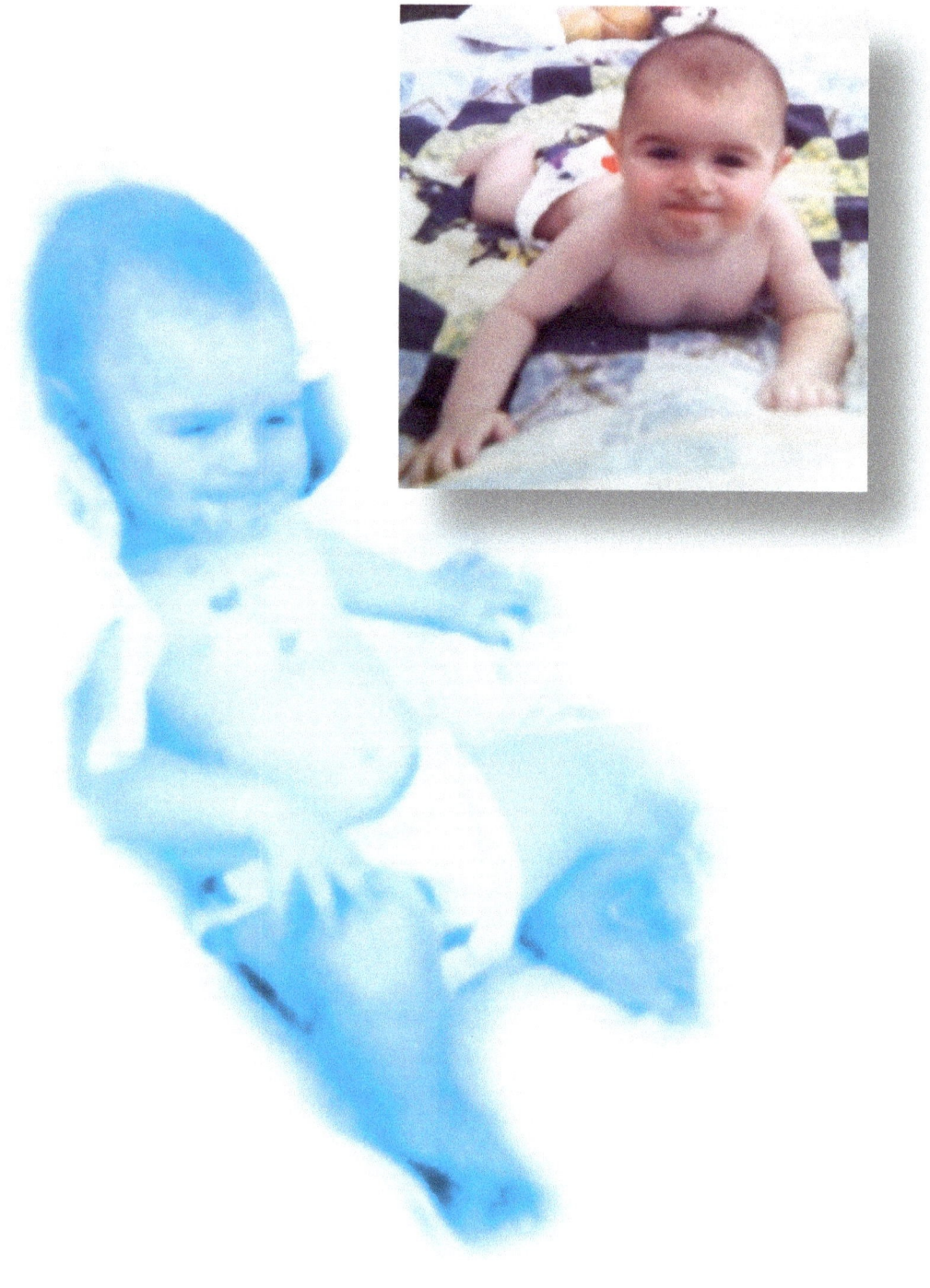

A note from Nana G,

Many years ago, in fact 25 years ago, my children and I would often head down to the local water hole out at Barney View in Queensland. We were blessed to own a gorgeous old Queenslander 2 mins away. We just loved the country life and everything it had to offer. When heading down to the water hole we would always pack a picnic lunch with us. This gave Tricky Nicky (approx 7 months at the time) the best opportunity to try his skills at feeding himself his favourite chocolate custard. These photos are of the day he tried with much passion and ended up in quite a state. That very same day I came up with this funny little story. Since leaving Barney View we still visit the area on occasions and go camping. I hope you enjoy my story.

Tricky Nicky's chocolate custard gets his mother very flustered. Custard here and custard there, custard, custard everywhere.

Chocolate custard on Nicky's nose,

chocolate custard between his toes.

On his hands and on his face,

all this custard all over the place.

Even custard on his eyelid.

What can you say about this kid?

Chocolate custard on his lip.

Oh, and look there's even some on his hip.

Chocolate custard in his hair, chocolate custard everywhere.

Chocolate custard in Nicky's hand,

chocolate custard in demand.

Chocolate custard on his chin,

oh Nick is a tricky thing.

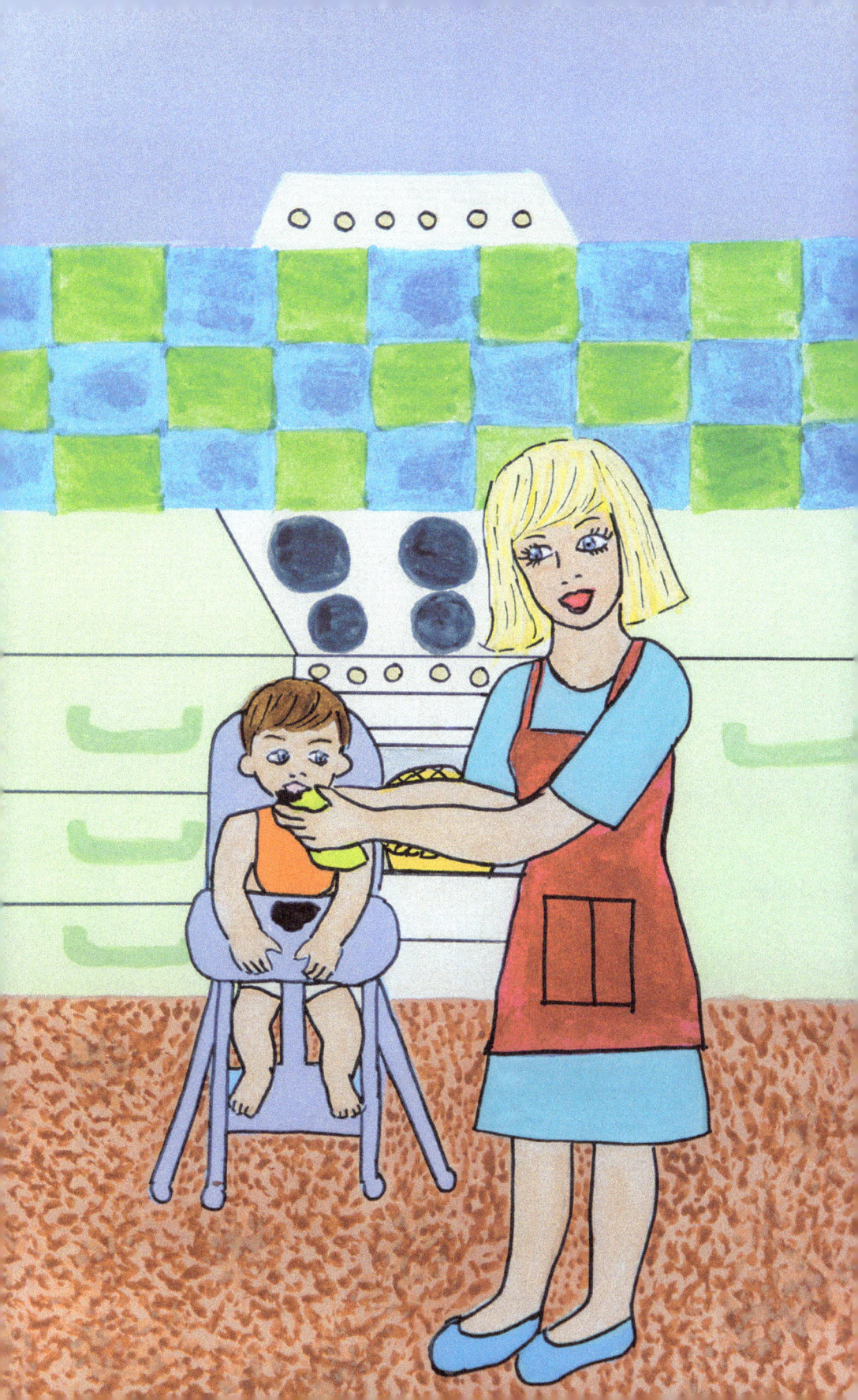

Chocolate custard on his ear,

isn't this custard in full gear?

Chocolate custard on Nick's feet,

wow, this custard is hard to beat.

Finally! Chocolate custard in the right place,

somewhere on his little face.

Chocolate custard, yes on his tongue.

Isn't custard lots of fun?

Great!! The custards been put down,

now poor mum don't need to frown.

Tricky Nick and his mum today

www.ingramcontent.com/pod-product-compliance
Lightning Source LLC
Chambersburg PA
CBHW062107290426
44110CB00022B/2738